ARIZONA II

ARIZONA II

PHOTOGRAPHY BY JOSEF MUENCH
TEXT BY TOM C. COOPER

Left: Montezuma's Head in the rugged Ajo Mountains,
emulates a silent sentinel as the light of day
makes its eternal transition.

International Standard Book Number 0-912856-48-3
Library of Congress Catalog Number 79-51787
Copyright© 1979 by Graphic Arts Center Publishing Co.
2000 N.W. Wilson • Portland, Oregon 97209 • 503/224-7777
Publisher • Charles H. Belding
Designer • Robert Reynolds
Printer • Graphic Arts Center
Typography • Paul O. Giesey/Adcrafters
Binding • Lincoln & Allen
Printed in the United States of America

Right: Light dusting of snow adheres to canyon wall at Bright Angel Point, on North Rim of Grand Canyon National Park.

ARIZONA II

The land we call Arizona has taken its share of knocks, and then some, both from nature and man. But the results are not bad at all.

Down through the millenniums, Mother Nature has tortured this place. The land has been inundated by seas, then cut by deep scars as waters made their downhill rush. Earthquakes have cracked, twisted, bent, heaved, folded and dropped this region. Volcanoes have erupted in every section of Arizona. And the land has suffered through extended periods of drought. If all this happened at once, Arizona would truly be a hell on earth.

But nature takes its time. And the torture handed out has come gradually over a period of four billion or so years.

Then, as if nature hadn't dealt enough blows, man added his. Some arrived in the form of harsh words. In the 1860s, when Arizona was fighting to win territorial status, a senator from Ohio remarked: "Oh, yes, I have heard of that country— it is just like hell. All it lacks is water and good society."

Kit Carson said Arizona was so poor that even a wolf would starve there, and in 1912 a California senator opposed Arizona's hopes for statehood with this innocuous remark: "You can't have statehood. You have too many Indians and Mormons there."

Despite all of these hard knocks, both verbal and physical, somebody likes Arizona. I do. I live there, and like it. So do thousands of others who have packed up and headed to Arizona looking for an oasis or rainbow. We can all report that Arizona is alive and doing quite well.

The Land

To know Arizona, you must first look at the land itself. It has been here, of course, throughout earth's history. So staggering is earth's lifespan of four billion years plus, that we cannot fully comprehend this much time. We can relate it in human terms, however, by compressing it into a 24-hour period. We begin at midnight. By breakfast time life appears in Arizona in the form of algae. By mid-afternoon, amphibians, reptiles and plant life appear. Soon dinosaurs become extinct. Mammals and birds develop. The drama that creates the Grand Canyon begins to unfold at approximately two minutes to midnight. With one and one-half minutes left in this 24-hour period, primitive man finally appears.

Man's recorded history, dating back 5000 years, begins at a mere two-fifths of a second remaining in this imaginary 24-hour period.

Incidently, as a state, Arizona is a youngster — having been admitted to the Union on Valentine's Day in 1912 as the 48th state. It is the sixth largest state, with a land mass of 113,909 square miles, almost twice the size of New England's six states. Its boundaries stretch 395 miles north to south, and 340 miles east to west.

This land we call Arizona can be divided into three distinct regions. Imagine a flight across the state beginning at Yuma, in the southwest corner, along the Colorado River. Arizona's lowest point is just 70 feet above sea level. You are in the low desert which occupies approximately one-third of the land. As your flight proceeds northeast, the land begins to rise, reaching 2500 feet at Tucson and 1000 feet at Phoenix. After heading over these two population centers, the land once again begins to rise, culminating at the Mogollon (moe-gee-on) Rim (the second region), a sharp 1000 to 2000 foot high escarpment that parades from the New Mexico border northwesterly to the Williams area, a distance of 200 miles. The land above this rim, over 5000 feet above sea level, is heavily forested and includes the largest stand of ponderosa pine in the world. This rim country then falls away gradually to the northeast and forms the Colorado Plateau (the third region) reaching to the four-corners area where Arizona, Utah, Colorado and New Mexico meet. The plateau is semi-arid or high desert composed of red rocks and soil. It represents about one-fifth of the land mass.

These three regions give Arizona a diversity that intrigues both the resident and the visitor. The desert environment is a separate world unto itself, with a fascinating plant and animal life that gives Arizona so much of its character. The forested region provides a contrasting element of pines, lakes and mountain streams, a very different world from that of the desert. The plateau seems somewhat out of place. It should logically fit between the desert and the mountain regions, but is instead a unique land, combining elements of the other two sections.

The Desert

The desert is a gaunt land, suggesting the fierce, defiant and struggling. It seems to be a battleground where the elements vie with one another for survival, reaching a crescendo in summer, when heat waves dance in the distance.

John C. Van Dyke, in *The Desert*, published by Charles Scribner's Sons in 1903, wrote that life on the desert is peculiarly savage. "It is a show of teeth in bush and beast and reptile. At every turn one feels the presence of the barb and thorn, the jaw and paw, the beak and talon, the sting and the poison thereof. Even the harmless Gila monster flattens his body on a rock and hisses a 'Don't step on me.' There is no living in concord or brotherhood here. Everything is at war with its neighbor, and the conflict is unceasing.

"Yet this conflict is not so obvious on the face of things. You hear no clash or crash or snarl. The desert is overwhelmingly silent. There is not a sound to be heard; and not a thing moves save the wind and the sands. But you look up at the worn peaks and the jagged barrancas, you look down at the wash-outs and piled boulders, you look about at the wind-tossed, half-starved bushes; and, for all the silence, you know that there is a struggle for life, a war for place, going on day by day."

Even today newcomers to the desert conjure up pictures of hissing poisonous snakes, bizarre plant life, and unbearable heat. The description fits. There *are* dangerous snakes in the Arizona desert. Plants *are* unusual and mystifying. And it *does* get hot (Arizona's all-time record high of 127 degrees was recorded at Parker in 1905).

The desert, perhaps more than any other type of land, has been romanticized, misunderstood and exaggerated. Others, like American statesman Daniel Webster discounted it: "What do we want with this vast, worthless area — this region of savages and wild beasts, of shifting sands and whirlwinds of dust, of cactus and prairie dogs? To what use could we even hope to put these great deserts and those endless mountain ranges?" Webster knew little about our desert.

On the other hand the late Joseph Wood Krutch, more than any other nature writer, has extolled the beauty and fascination of Arizona's desert lands. "Those who have never known it are to be pitied, like a man who has never read *Hamlet* or heard the *Jupiter Symphony*. He has missed something which is unique. And there is nothing else which can give him more than a hint of what he has missed. To have experienced it is to be prepared to see other landscapes with new eyes and to participate with a fresh understanding in the life of other natural communities."

There are others who are quick to point out that some of the world's great religions were born in desert regions. They refer specifically to Christianity and Judaism. Perhaps there is an aura about the desert which borders on religious experience. Many believe so.

Technically speaking, the scientific world defines a desert as a region subjected to high temperatures and the recipient of less than ten inches of annual precipitation. Elevation and the distance from the equator are major factors, as are winds, mountains and ocean currents which affect the climate of the arid lands.

Geologically speaking, deserts are relative newcomers in the life of this planet. Some scientists believe they are as new as 5 million years. Others date deserts at 50 to 60 million years. At various times, geologists claim, the Arizona desert regions were inundated by seas, which left behind deep-lying layers of limestone. On the surface soils are sandy, ranging from very fine material to coarse. Contrary to popular belief, these soils are capable of supporting plant life, providing there is sufficient moisture.

There are four desert regions in the United States, and all four are found in Arizona. Much of the state's southern and southwestern region is in the Sonoran Desert shared by Arizona and the Mexican state of Sonora. The Chihuahuan Desert, found mostly in Mexico, touches the southeast corner of Arizona. The Great Basin Desert includes the northeast part of the state, known as the Colorado Plateau. The fourth desert region is the Mohave Desert, in which California's Death Valley is located. This desert touches the northwestern corner of Arizona.

The Sonoran Desert, covering 12,000 square miles in Arizona, a tip of California and part of Mexico, is the dominant desert in Arizona. It is here that Arizona's trademark, the giant saguaro (sa-war-oh) cactus reigns. Its statuesque appearance, with arms stretching skyward, is a thing of natural beauty, particularly when silhouetted against a setting sun. It is a sight that beckons people to the desert time and time again. I suppose, next to the Grand Canyon, the saguaro is the most photographed subject in Arizona.

The life story of the saguaro is fascinating. It took years of study just to determine how the giant succulent propogates itself. The flower, which is Arizona's official flower, produces large pollen grains which are transported by birds and bees to carry on cross-pollination. The creamy white flower may open once after sundown, usually in late May or June, and then close forever in a matter of a day or so. Each saguaro produces approximately four or five flowers a day, for a period of 30 days.

During the mature lifespan of the giant, it is calculated that each saguaro produces 12 million seeds. Only *one* must germinate and reach maturity to maintain a constant balance of plants. In some areas of the desert the equilibrium is off balance, and the number of plants is slowly diminishing, an alarming fact which some scientists attribute to minute changes in our climate.

If a seed is to sprout at all when summer rains come (two rains within a five-day period greatly enhance the seed's hopes), it must overcome incredible difficulties. The tiny black seed must germinate in partial shade, and have optimum temperatures around 77 degrees F. If no shade is available or the temperature drops to about 60 or climbs to 95 degrees, chances of germination are greatly diminished. Finally, the tiny seed must somehow avoid hungry birds and animals which also take their toll. As you can see, the odds for a saguaro seed to reach a point where it can take root are rather slim. Because of their need for delicate balancing of shade, moisture and temperature and threat of being eaten by natural predators, only about one percent of the seeds that do germinate ever reach any substantial growth.

If the seedling somehow survives these almost incredible odds, it will take nine or ten years before the plant reaches a height of six inches. After 25 years, it may stand three to four feet high. Branches or arms usually develop as the cactus reaches ten or more feet and about 75 years of age. Most saguaros will reach 35 feet after 150 years, with some living up to 200 years, perhaps topping out at nearly 40 feet.

A mature saguaro has an extensive lateral root system that fans out around the plant at a distance approximately equal to its height. A small tap root develops, but it is the wide-spreading root system which absorbs most of the moisture when it rains. Thanks to its pleated structure, the plant can expand to take up large quantities of water for use during dry periods. Thus it bulges following rains, and shrinks during dry periods, as the plant utilizes the stored moisture.

The greatest danger confronting the saguaro population is man himself. It is appalling to see so many saguaros near roadways heavily scared by vandals. A plant that has been around for 100 years and more can be quickly doomed by such damage in a matter of minutes.

Replacing the giants is a frustrating task. After all, if you produce a seedling in a nursery today, it will take half a century or more before the plant achieves much growth. Some of us won't be around that long. The Saguaro National Monument, with two sections, one on the eastside of Tucson and another on the westside, show marked differences in self-propogation. In the east section, very little new growth is apparent, but in the western part large stands of young saguaros reach forest densities. The reason for the differences is not yet clear.

Another federally operated park is Organ Pipe National Monument west of Tucson and south of Gila Bend. The organ pipe cactus, appropriately named, grows in great numbers there on the Arizona-Mexico border.

The yucca, a member of the lily family, is another unique desert plant. It sports sword-like leaves and produces a large stock topped by flowers. It has its own private arrangement with a moth, an arrangement beneficial to both parties. When a yucca blooms, it depends on an inch-long moth to fertilize the flower, which cannot be fertilized in any other way. The female moth collects a ball of pollen from one flower and then takes it to another. There she inserts her egg tube into the pistil and injects several eggs. She then climbs on top of the flower, leaves her pollen ball and makes sure that the pollen is properly deposited. She derives no benefit whatsoever from this chore.

After fertilization takes place, yucca flowers wither and die. The larvae then hatch, bore their way out of the plant, drop to the ground, and dig into the soil where they spin cocoons, and eventually transform themselves into adult moths which repeat the cycle the next year.

And the yucca lives on. There is virtually no way of explaining how this arrangement came about. It is a mystery of the desert which we will probably never unravel. I'm content enough just to know that such things do happen in the Arizona desert, and feel richer for knowing it.

Plants adapt to the strenuous desert environment in numerous ways. The prickly pear cactus is composed of water conserving "pads" instead of branches; the cholla (choy-ya) sports thousands of spines or needles for shade and protection; and the mesquite bush will sink roots 200 feet deep in search of moisture, as one startled underground miner discovered several years ago. The barrel cactus, like the saguaro, has a pleated structure so it may expand and store water. The ocotillo (oh-coh-tee-yo) sprouts leaves on its spindly branches after a rain, then they quickly dry out and fall off. In addition to the leaves, the ocotillo sports a cluster of flowers at the tip of its branches. The slow growing ironwood tree justifies its name. It will discourage anyone from using an axe; even those with a chain saw are amazed at the density and toughness of the tree.

Spring can be a flamboyant season for the desert. If sufficient rain has fallen (remember the desert averages only seven to ten inches annually) and temperatures are right, the desert will reward visitors with an extravaganza of flowers. Poppies may reach carpet-like densities with large orange colored petals. Lupine, with its showy blue flowers, will line roadways for miles.

If the moisture-temperature ratio is just right, the desert explodes with color, transforming it into an Eden. The profusion of color and new life is limited, however, for summer temperatures of 100 degrees or more daily dries the plants, allowing seeds to fall to the ground to await another spring.

Pet areas for eyeing desert flowers are along Apache Trail, east of Phoenix (State 88), Picacho Peak area, 40 miles northwest of Tucson (Interstate 10), Kitt Peak area, west of Tucson (State 86) and Florence to Tucson highway (U.S. 89).

Reptiles, animals and birds also have various means of adapting to the harsh desert environment. During the heat of summer, a rattlesnake will seek shade during the day and feed during the cooler night hours. The kangaroo rat never drinks water, even if it's available. Instead, this small rodent has developed an amazing ability to break down the carbohydrates of seeds for its moisture.

The cactus wren hides its nest amid the sharp spines of a cholla cactus. It must sit down upon its nest very carefully!

The transition from day to night is a most memorable experience on the desert. Once I was shooting photographs of a majestic sunset from the east side of Tucson. Occasionally I heard the yipping of a coyote or two, but paid little attention because of my concentration on picture-taking. As the last rays of the sun dropped below the horizon, I sat down to soak up the lingering color in the sky, and found myself surrounded by coyotes. I was relatively new to the desert and didn't know much about these wily critters. So I was especially uncertain about their attitude toward humans, and admit to being somewhat apprehensive, particularly because I was about a quarter-mile from the safety of my car. It was rapidly getting dark, so I began a fast walk out to the roadway, the coyotes following, maintaining their circle around me. Despite the uncertainty, I began to savor their sounds ... once I was near the car. I waited. The coyotes yipped for several minutes, and gradually grew quiet. Then, seemingly bored with me, the pack went about more serious matters.

I later learned that coyotes aren't about to tackle man, and grew to relish sounds made by them near my prior home in Tucson. Their barking is a haunting, dramatic desert sound.

On another occasion, I awoke to find seven inches of snow on the ground—in Tucson! It isn't supposed to snow on the desert, particularly when winter visitors from colder climes are visiting Arizona. It snowed anyway.

I quickly dressed, grabbed my camera gear and raced into the desert a few miles from home. I rapidly exhausted my supply of film on this unusual sight, and stood for awhile absorbing the visual drama before me. The desert was absolutely quiet. Birds did not fly. Animals did not move. It was an eerie quiet.

Perhaps they were so startled at the sight of snow they were mesmerized.

In true form for a winter paradise, the snow melted rapidly and was completely gone by noon. Tender desert plants and winter visitors were probably grateful.

It was a rare event, and the snow got national publicity, much to the chagrin of Arizona's tourist industry.

One last note on the desert involves the matter of rains. In an area so unaccustomed to moisture, it seems that the desert doesn't know what to do when it does storm. The rocky-sandy soil has very little capacity to absorb rains, which often come as sudden downpours lasting only minutes. When such a cloudburst develops, dry meandering streambeds can become nightmares of flashflooding, the result of heavy runoff from nearby hills or mountains. It can be a real threat to property and to unsuspecting motorists attempting to drive through the usually dry washes.

The reputation of the desert as being inhospitable or brutal can be real for a tourist who must step out of an air-conditioned automobile at a rest stop in the desert during a July or August afternoon. The scene is uninviting. The sun and heat are relentless, and there is little visible greenery. It can be a most unpleasant experience. Unfortunately, many people see the desert only under such conditions. They miss the other three seasons, or the desert at sunrise or sunset. To really experience the lure of the desert, you must see her in all her moods. Then and only then, can you come to love the desert, and perhaps understand it. Krutch again, writing in *The Voice of the Desert,* concluded, "Long before I ever saw the desert, I was aware of the mystical overtones which the observation of nature made audible to me. But I have never been more frequently or more vividly aware of them than in connection with the desert phenomena."

Before leaving the desert, I remember standing among saguaros in brutal summer heat, hearing small gusts of wind piercing the silence. These gusts whisper through the spiny needles of cactus. It is a haunting sound which seems to exemplify the mystique of this land.

Ironically, it is the same sound I hear as winds whisper through the needles of Arizona's forested highlands.

The Highlands

Every pine-covered area in this country has a resort or vacation hideaway called "Whispering Pines." Arizona is no exception. The pines do whisper and beckon visitors, newcomers and natives to the higher elevations for a reward which the desert cannot give—green meadows and forested hills, cool air, and vistas that seem endless. You might call it "Arizona's other world."

Graphically speaking, Arizona's uplands or highlands can be divided into two classes. First, there are the "islands in the sky"—mountains that rear up out of the desert to elevations of 9000 feet or more above sea level. These are the Santa Catalinas, Santa Ritas, the Rincons near Tucson and the Pinalenos near Safford. Then there are ranges rising out of areas more than a mile high: Bill Williams Mountain west of Flagstaff, the San Francisco Peaks north of Flagstaff and the Chuska Mountains in the northeast corner of the state.

It is such mountains as these, that, when contrasted against the desert lands give Arizona such an incredible diversity.

You can begin a hike north of Tucson's desert hillsides dotted with saguaros and wind your way up 9157-foot Mt. Lemmon, through seven different life zones. When you reach the top you will find yourself in a climatic zone common to northern Minnesota or southern Canada.

In winter you can enjoy a brunch at a Tucson resort in 70-degree weather, then drive to Mt. Lemmon in 60 minutes and ski its north side. That's variety made free, by nature.

Two-thirds of Arizona's population lives on the desert lands surrounding the Phoenix and Tucson areas. The highlands are their summer retreat, a place to go in winter to remind them of "back home"—in Indiana, Iowa or North Dakota.

The bulk of Arizona's highlands is a dog-bone shaped region, running from the New Mexico border northwestward for 200 miles. This is a heavily forested land, the biggest part of which is known as the White Mountains. This is an area about 20,000 square miles composed of small lakes, mountain streams, meadows and dense forests of aspen and pine. It also gives rise to four prominent rivers, the Little Colorado, the Black, the White, and the Salt.

It is a land of ranching, forestry and recreation. And it's home to the White Mountain Apache. Much of their reservation land has been developed for tourism. Here you can find 26 lakes, 300 miles of trout streams, and nearly a thousand different campgrounds. The tribe also owns Sunrise Lodge, a relatively new motel with 106 rooms, a convention hall for 200 persons, a restaurant, bar, swimming pool, sauna, Jacuzzi, gift shop and nearby at least 15 ski runs.

Also, numerous summer home developments have sprung up in this area since the 1950s.

These mountains, while summer and winter playgrounds, are a year around essential for the million-plus residents of the metropolitan Phoenix area. For it is from these mountains the Salt River flows, the lifeline for the desert valley. A series of impoundments or reservoirs stores runoff from snow and rain and is gradually lowered into canals snaking across the desert floor in and about Phoenix.

Much of the White Mountain region not a part of the Apache Reservation is regulated by the U.S. Forest Service and the Bureau of Land Management. Grazing and recreational development are directed by both federal agencies, as is harvesting the world's largest stand of ponderosa pine.

The mountains mean different things to different people.

My two sons and I pulled into a Hawley Lake campground after dark one summer evening. Because of the late hour, we cooked inside our trailer. My youngest son, age 10 at the time, and a budding astronomer, walked outside after dinner and looked up. "Dad, Dad," he shouted. "Look!" I ran outside not knowing what to expect. He stared skyward. He was seeing the Milky Way for the first time, clearly etched across the sky. The stars seemed to dance.

We were at 9000 feet in the uplands, amid cool, clear air.

This land is also Zane Grey country. From his mountain cabin Grey penned some of his best works: *Riders of the Purple Sage,* and its sequel, *The Rainbow Trail.* Grey's romance with Arizona began in 1906. In the peak of his career in Arizona he earned $650,000 a year from his writing. His cabin home, and the vista from its porch are still there to see.

Spring comes to the White Mountains very slowly. Warmer temperatures take their toll of the snow, first exposing small patches of soil which slowly grow wider, and then in just a few days creating forests of lush new growth. But the seasons in the mountains can be fickle. Just when you think winter has gone into a deep sleep, winds can churn out of the northwest and drop their cargo of the white fluffy stuff. But it's only a temporary setback. Spring quickly returns, perhaps even the next day and begins the melting job all over.

Streams, seemingly dormant during the winter, jump with life. The runoff from melting snow and sporadic rains may swell them to brimful and maybe more. Flowers prepare for their summer show. Wildlife begins to frolic. It's like being born all over again.

Summer in the highlands is heralded by the arrival of either desert dwellers or warmer temperatures, usually both. Anglers take to the streams and lakes. Summer-home owners open their cabins and cottages for the season. And traffic picks up on the roads winding through the forest.

Everywhere it's green and quite cool. It's like another world.

Fall slips in slowly through the forests and along the streams. Aspen leaves slowly turn gold, the color first appearing in the highest elevations around Mt. Baldy and Escudilla. Then Autumn's extravaganza slowly moves down toward the lower elevations along the Rim. The Coronado Trail (U.S. Route 666) along the eastern border of Arizona is a real fall color show-off. The road parallels the route taken by Coronado in 1540 in his unsuccessful search for the Seven Cities of Cibola. If he had made the trip in the fall, he would have found gold all along the trail, aspen gold.

Fall lingers. But slowly, cooler breezes move in over the mountains, leaves drop, and warm weather plants retreat to wait for another spring revival.

Winter creeps in and grips the forest, sometimes mercilessly. Campers and motor homes are replaced by cars with skis fastened atop. Ice fishermen arrive. Christmas-tree hunters prowl the areas set aside by the Forest Service, proving that winter is not all bad.

This forested belt along the Mogollon Rim runs northwest from the White Mountains toward Flagstaff and Williams. It also swings southwest to join the Sedona and Prescott areas.

Flagstaff, a focal point along Interstate 40, looms up at 6900 feet above sea level, watched over by the San Francisco Peaks, a group of three mountains left over from ancient volcanic action: Humphrey's Peak, the highest elevation in Arizona, topping out at 12,633 feet, and Agassiz and Fremont.

There is a certain alpine flavor to Flagstaff. Pine and aspen are mixed with volcanic debris. Many homes have a pile of firewood stacked in the yard. And on a cold winter night you can smell the burning pine for miles.

As you near the city from Phoenix on Interstate 17, you climb 6000 feet over the 140 mile route, from low desert, through high desert, then grasslands and finally forest.

The city, with a population of 35,000, is the hub of northern Arizona and is the gateway to the Grand Canyon and the vast Indian lands in the northeast section of Arizona. Northern Arizona University, with an enrollment of 13,000, is located on the south edge of Flagstaff. It experienced explosive growth in the 1970s, due partly to the influx of students from the desert communities of Tucson and Phoenix who wanted to find something different. Many found it, all right. During the winter of 1967-68, about 100 inches of snow fell on the city in a matter of days. One of Arizona's major ski areas, the Snow Bowl, is on the west slope of the San Francisco Peaks.

Approximately 30 miles west of Flagstaff is the town of Williams and 9,268 foot Bill Williams Mountain. The mountain and the San Francisco Peaks were like beacons on the horizon, helping settlers navigate this country in the 1800s.

South of Williams, the forested belt takes you around the west side of Sedona and on into the Prescott area. Here the Bradshaw Mountains reign.

There also are isolated forest areas in the Chuska Mountains in the northeast corner of the state, atop the Santa Catalinas and the Santa Ritas near Tucson, and around Mt. Graham near Safford.

These timbered lands, while providing another climate for Arizona, also represent an annual $175 million wood products industry. They add even another dimension to the face of Arizona, one which is usually overlooked. If you tell friends living in other parts of the nation that you're spending the summer in Arizona, they might send you a sympathy card. Many do not realize that we Arizonans can retreat into our air-conditioned home, car and office, or the mountains where nature provides a cool breeze whispering through the pines.

The High Desert

Arizona's third land region is the Colorado Plateau, the Great Basin lying northeast of the Mogollon Rim. The forested Mogollon Rim, which scallops its way across the state, divides the low desert from the high desert. Here the elevations slope away from the Rim's 7000 feet down to 5500 feet.

This is the land of the Grand Canyon, the Colorado River and its little brother, the Painted Desert and Petrified Forest. The land of colored sandstone monoliths rising a thousand feet or more above the plain robed in hues of brown and red.

Vistas across this sprawling region are awesome.

Other states have deserts. Still others have forests. But only Arizona and Utah offer so many startling land forms as found on this plateau.

It truly is a land of staggering beauty.

The boundaries of the Great Basin Desert are difficult to define, but it encompasses parts of Idaho, Oregon, a tip of Nevada, a sliver of Colorado and Wyoming, nearly all of Utah and about 20,000 square miles of Arizona.

Like other deserts, this land was once an ancient sea bed. What is left now is sand—virtually everywhere—in wrinkled dunes and tightly compacted sandstone rock.

Time and weather have shaped this region, the elements chiseling away in a process old as time. The most pronounced features of this land are the mesas and the scattering of towering monoliths. Monument Valley on the Arizona-Utah border is one of the classic creations.

The beauty of this land is astounding, because of wind sculptured sand dunes, broad mesas and towering sandstone monuments, all red. Many motion pictures have been made here. One portion of the valley is even called Ford's Point, after movie director John Ford.

Plant and animal life are delicately balanced in Monument Valley. Where today pinyon and juniper trees struggle against the dry winds, grass once grew, two to three feet high, and as recently as 50 years ago. "Grass grew as high as a horse's belly. All over this place," a Navajo friend told me. Then flocks of sheep gradually whittled away at it, and now you find only small patches which have escaped overgrazing.

But the land is still eager. Evidence has revealed early Indian inhabitants of this area grew squash, corn and even cotton.

The Hopi Indians, who live on mesas in the middle of this region, carefully cultivate small corn crops, watermelons and peaches on sandy soil below their villages, and hand plant the corn with sticks as they have done for centuries, for corn is essential to many of their religious ceremonies. The Hopis believe in harmonizing with nature, which may be why they seem to be able to breathe life into this soil.

Nearly 120 miles south of Monument Valley is the heart of Painted Desert and Petrified Forest. It is a national park, with headquarters along Interstate 40, 20 miles east of Holbrook.

Here you'll find prehistoric trees, some up to 250 feet in length, seemingly "frozen" in rock form. The jeweled stone-logs are an astonishing sight.

The park preserves the greatest concentration of petrified wood known to man, in a natural area surrounded by the many hued Painted Desert. Together, they attract several hundred thousand visitors annually.

The area of petrified wood and colorful soils is located in what geologists call the Chinle formation. (You'll find many fossils, in addition to the "wood" in this region.) Actually, the Chinle formation consists of various rock types, from soft, fine-grained material to the harder more coarsely grained, providing a startling array of color variations. Colors are known to shift abruptly as you walk through the area and are especially bright after a rain. Here the rain also causes large scale erosion which makes the Painted Desert similar in appearance to the Badlands of South Dakota. The erosion cycle continues as it has for millions of years, continually exposing new fossils and petrified wood.

Two hundred million years ago the Petrified Forest was a swamp or marsh filled with plant and animal life. It consisted of low-lying mud banks, sand bars and ponds cut by rivers or streams which fluctuated between cycles of wet and dry. These streams, it is thought, carried many logs into the area, some of which caught in mud or entanglements of their own making. Under normal circumstances they would have deteriorated and returned their elements back to the soil. But here, something happened to the logs, what, scientists are not certain. Some believe that the swampy areas covered by water caused a slower rate of deterioration because the oxygen needed for decay was not present. The silica-laden water filtered through the bark of the logs, eventually separated from the solution and formed small crystals of quartz within the plants' tissues.

Two types of petrification then resulted. In one instance, the quartz crystals filled in the plant's cells without any further change taking place. Thus, the resulting petrified wood accurately resembled the original log. In other cases, the growing quartz crystals dissolved in the cell walls of the entire log without maintaining any detail.

The water which supplied silica for the petrification process also added other minerals: iron, copper, manganese and carbon, all producing various colors. Therefore, a piece of petrified wood can be extremely colorful, typifying the precious beauty only nature and time can produce.

The late afternoon sun plays beautifully on the massive jeweled logs and the surrounding Painted Desert. Colors become magnified as the lingering sunlight pierces the atmosphere, and the hills, with their own hues of the rainbow, take on an added glow. Sunset is a fitting tribute to nature's drama played out in this wide-open, wind-swept region.

The Grandest Canyon

No one person can aptly describe the Grand Canyon, but observing visitors as they first sight the canyon's depths and listening to their remarks, says a lot about this place.

"Oh, my God."

"So *this* is it. I *don't* believe it," another says quietly.

But others are absolutely still, staring hynotically or shaking their heads . . . in disbelief.

I once stood on Hopi Point preparing to set up my camera to photograph some of the late afternoon light on the canyon walls. There were only four of us, my wife and I, and another couple a few feet away. It was silent, except for two things:

the muffled roar of the Colorado River nearly three miles away, and the sound of the lady occasionally turning a page in a book. It was the bible.

She read to herself.

He stared.

About half an hour before sunset a busload of tourists arrived. They were noisy as they approached the viewing point, then the noise subsided. There was a sense of reverence . . . of being overwhelmed . . . awestruck.

Finally, the drama of this special experience began to wane as the sun moved beyond the horizon.

The couple was undaunted by the departing group. He continued to gaze into the canyon depths and she read. As the bus left I picked up my camera gear and got into my car. I waited, I hated to start the engine. Finally, I did turn the ignition key. The engine started, it seemed so noisy . . . noisier than ever before. I pulled away and glanced back. They were still there.

That couple really existed. I haven't any notion how long they might have remained. But they typify the power that the Grand Canyon casts upon mortals.

Sunrise and sunset are special times of the day in this enchanted place. In the morning the horizon slowly glows into a bright image, and then the sun blasts through and floods the canyon with long shadows and red light, then yellow light and shorter shadows. Eventually the whole scene rushes into the brilliance of a new day.

You can bet there are people out there somewhere on both rims filled with exaltation. And there are those who totally miss the significance. They amble to the rim expecting a loud show of light and form. Their loss is the spiritual and visual stimulation that only this canyon can impart. For most it is a very real thing . . . something that brings people back . . . again . . . and again.

Like Josef Muench, a photographic connoisseur who has made more than 190 trips in 42 years to capture the visual mysteries of this majestic place says, "I know why I come back. I can't explain it, but I know. Perhaps some of my photos speak louder than my words." Both his words and photos speak out in tribulation to the most colossal natural wonder on this planet.

For the faithful, there are never two sunrises or sunsets alike. Each seems different in the way the sun's rays and the resulting shadows play on the land forms.

Arizona's native senator and presidential candidate, Barry Goldwater, is a man in love with this land. He talks about his feelings: "When I first walked up to the rim of the Grand Canyon when I was 7 or 8 years old, I felt then and have felt many times since that I opened my eyes and saw the hand of God . . . there is an ethereal something that runs through my mind . . . looking into the depths down to the schists through which the river flows . . . realizing that that dark block of rock formed the base of mountains which once were taller than the Alps. You can look at the river from a mile above, cruise its quiet and rough waters, camp by its side on a moonlit night and listen to the stories the waters tell you.

"What's the best way to see the canyon? Get up in the morning an hour before dawn, and with your camera go to the rim and sit and sit and sit. Look and look for one whole day, until the canyon again is dark.

"Then, my friend, you have lived."

Frank Waters, a New Mexico author with brilliant credentials also speaks eloquently of this wonder of creation. "The Grand Canyon is the sum total of all the aspects of nature combined in one integrated whole. It is at once the smile and frown upon the face of nature. In its heart is the savage, uncontrollable fury of all the inanimate universe, and at the same time the immeasurable serenity that succeeds it.

"It is creation."

Presidents, premiers, cosmonauts and astronauts, kings and queens have come to the canyon. Some haven't had much to say, which speaks well of the canyon, too. But Teddy Roosevelt let go with a succinct statement: "Absolutely unparalleled throughout the world."

Writer-philosopher Joseph Wood Krutch called the canyon: "The most revealing single page of the earth's history anywhere open on the face of the globe."

People and nations will argue forever as to which of the seven wonders of the world is *the* wonder. It would be only verbal gymnastics to enter such a contest. Suffice it to say, they are all great . . . wonders, if you please. But for me, the Grand Canyon holds a special place. It is enough. And as you learn more about the canyon, emotions and gut reactions become even stronger and more meaningful.

Technically speaking, the canyon is the most severe scar in the earth's crust. It runs 280 miles, mostly east to west, as measured along the Colorado River. Its width measures from 4 to 18 miles, depending upon where you measure. The most widely seen area, around the north and south rim villages, is a gap approximately nine miles wide.

If you want to gain a quick appreciation for the meaning of "canyon", take a flight from Grand Canyon Airport. You'll skim out over the trees . . . and then over the rim. Suddenly the land drops several thousand feet in an instant. It's enough to make your stomach jump into your throat.

And then down, under the rim . . . down . . . you're a thousand feet *below* your airport!

The canyon begins to become meaningful in size and scale.

Or try hiking down from the North Rim and up to the South Rim. It's a good way to see the canyon. And feel it. For most (after some warnings about stress and strain for unconditioned hikers) a hike down one day and out the next is enough. You can also ride muleback. Either way, the experience is unforgettable.

Others are content to helicopter over, down, around and through, finally out of the awesome phenomenon.

Perhaps the most intimidating, yet exciting, experiences within the Grand Canyon is to traverse the park by boat or raft on the mighty Colorado River. It is the river, of course, which has partially created this yawning canyon.

During the period of white man's exploration of the river, beginning in the 1860s until shortly after World War II, fewer than 100 persons were known to have made the river trip through the canyon. Today, a closely regulated 16,000 people a year go through. To many, it is the ultimate way to experience the canyon.

No discussion of the Grand Canyon would be complete without looking at the creation of this natural wonder. It transcends even the wildest imagination. It should also be noted that the grandest of canyons is still the subject of numerous scientific studies, making it the most thoroughly examined canyon in the world.

Most geologists agree that the canyon itself is only 8 to 10 million years old, but this only accounts for the amount of time it has taken the Colorado River to carve this spectacle. The bedrock, from which the canyon is carved, is something else again, its several layers date back about two billion years, roughly half of the life span of earth.

The base layer of the canyon apparently was once a region of mountains ranging as high as 18,000 feet. It took about half a billion years of erosion to create a plain approximating sea level. Evidence of this plain is visible along the river today.

The next layer of material was created by tidal pools, oceans, rivers and even volcanoes. Evidence shows that this level also developed into mountains which, like the previous layer, were subjected to erosion from which another plain developed. In the next period, the region dipped and heaved over millions of years. Several times the land was below sea level and filled with water. During other geologic periods the land was raised and waters sought paths to the lower level of the seas. Finally the oceans returned once more as the land subsided. You can study the unique evidence of this final

invasion in the uppermost limestone layers along the rims.

Between 60 and 65 million years ago, the area was a low plateau covering portions of Arizona, Colorado, Utah and New Mexico. Finally parts of this plateau were raised to nearly 10,000 feet above sea level, corresponding very closely to the present elevation of the North Rim.

The etching of the canyon by water and wind is the next chapter. We already know the canyon was carved by the river which eventually was named the Colorado. Supplied by the waters from a large drainage area extending into Utah and Colorado, the river took a route to the seas by wearing and cutting through rocks offering the least resistance. Why the river selected this particular route is still somewhat of a mystery. Today the wearing and cutting process continues. Spectacular examples of this process are visible in many of the lower reaches of the canyon and along the river.

The river that formed this canyon also is a mazy subject in itself. It rises in the high elevations of Colorado's Rocky Mountains, draining nearly a quarter of a million square miles, and enters the Gulf of California, a span of 1450 miles.

Numerous tributaries feed into the Colorado. The Green River, beginning in Wyoming, runs approximately 700 miles until it empties into the Colorado in Canyonlands National Park in Utah. The San Juan River from Colorado also joins the Colorado just above the Arizona border.

Merrill D. Beal, a career employee with the National Park Service and at one time chief park naturalist at the Grand Canyon, estimated the staggering power of the Colorado River through the canyon. Writing in *Grand Canyon, The Story Behind the Scenery* (published by KC Publications, Las Vegas, Nevada 89114), Beal estimated that the river can carry from a few hundred tons a day, during low water levels, up to 27 million tons per day during a flood such as the one which occurred in 1927. Beal estimated that over a period of several years the river averaged a load of sand and silt of nearly 400,000 tons a day.

Putting these figures into more meaningful terms, Beal points out that if the 400,000-ton average burden were loaded into five-ton capacity dump trucks, it would take 80,000 trucks hauling at a rate of less than one per second for 24 hours to equal the amount of work done by the river! These gargantuan figures are for suspended material only. The river also moves rocks and boulders along the stream-bed for great distances, which, again according to Beal, might equal the load of suspended material!

These figures apply to the uncontrolled Colorado River as it was before the construction of the Hoover Dam, at the west end of the canyon in the 1930s. It was built to store water from the Colorado River and to generate electrical power. Hoover Dam created 110-mile long Lake Mead. Once waters slow down in a lake-like environment, sediment or suspended materials begin to settle out. Thus, the lake fills with sand and silt, eventually spelling doom for itself.

Upstream from the canyon, Lake Powell (named for explorer John Wesley Powell) was created in 1963 when Glen Canyon Dam was finished and began controlling waters of the upper Colorado. The dam project on the Arizona-Utah border was very controversial, primarily because it caused rising lake waters to flood dozens of magnificent side canyons. Glen Canyon Dam now catches about 80 percent of the sediment carried by the Colorado and is obviously on a course of self-destruction as Lake Powell fills itself with sand and silt. Estimates of the dam's useful life vary widely, and the project is still shrouded in controversy.

The water being released from Glen Canyon Dam is relatively clear and sometimes has a greenish hue when it moves through the Grand Canyon because the sediment has settled out. But when the Paria River or the Little Colorado River (tributaries below Glen Canyon Dam) are running, they deposit a brownish color into the big Colorado.

So the mighty Colorado has been somewhat tamed by man

and now serves as a workhorse, generating electrical power and providing great quantities of water for parts of Arizona's and California's agriculture. Further, when the controversial Central Arizona Project is completed in the 1980s, river water will flow through a massive aqueduct to Phoenix . . . that is, if there is sufficient funding to complete the project, and the Colorado has enough water left.

By the time the river reaches the Gulf of California, it is spent. Large deltas have fanned out from the mouth. At certain periods, not even a trickle may reach the gulf.

Though man has harnessed this great river, ask someone who has taken a raft or boat trip through the Grand Canyon if the river is really tamed. They can tell you hair-raising stories about violent rapids which pitch large rafts about as though they were toys. But you needn't run the river to sense the majesty of the Colorado, just stand quietly on the South Rim of the canyon someday and listen carefully. You can hear the roar of the river's rapids nearly three miles away!

As you stand on the rims of the Grand Canyon and gaze into the rocky depths, you usually are not aware of the many plants and animals that exist there. Your gaze is taken up with the canyon's imponderable dimensions.

But life abounds within the canyon.

For example, there are known to be 220 kinds of birds and about 100 different kinds of animals in the national park, including beavers, bighorn sheep, lizards, mule deer, porcupines, mountain lions, snakes, pronghorn antelope, fox, spotted skunk and non-native wild burros.

Due to the creation of the canyon, which split the land into two distinct areas, some evolutionary changes have taken place in animals, creating two species from one. An interesting example is squirrels found in the park. They are of two varieties, although biologists believe they were once one. On the North Rim is found the Kaibab squirrel, with black underparts and a white tail. The South Rim is home for the Abert squirrel, with large ears, grey body and tail, and white underparts. Yet, both are separated by only a few miles.

At the river level, the climate is much like a desert, where you can find broiling summer temperatures and an average rainfall of about 10 inches. Here you will find several types of cactus along with delphiniums, poppies and white thistles.

The North Rim, averaging 1200 feet higher than the South Rim, is heavily forested with pine and aspen. The South Rim sports juniper and pinyon-type vegetation. And because the North Rim is higher, it is common to find several feet of snow on the ground in winter while the lower South Rim may get several inches of snow lasting only a day or so.

Such is the variety of this agape Grand Canyon region.

Man in the Grand Canyon

Imagine living in the earth's deepest and most colorful canyon and growing accustomed to the spectacular sights at one's front door! The experience is difficult for me to comprehend. But man was living in the Grand Canyon as early as 4000 years ago, a fact scientists have deduced from the dwellings located in the canyon's walls.

The Navajo, living to the east of the Grand Canyon, have a legend which explains how it developed. The legend says that continued rains resulted in a massive flood which inundated the area to great depths. To survive, they believe that the early people were temporarily turned into fish. Finally, an outlet for this massive flood developed the Grand Canyon, permitting the water to drain away.

A few Navajos will not eat fish because of this legend.

The first white men to see the canyon were Spanish conquistadors. Hopi Indians living a hundred or so miles to the east led part of Coronado's expedition to the rim in 1540, but did not show them how to reach the river far below.

The second white visitors to the canyon were Spanish padres on July 2 or 3, 1776. In the 1820s American fur trappers were next to arrive at the canyon. But white men took their first serious look at the canyon in 1857-58 when Lt. Joseph Ives led a War Department expedition to examine the river to determine its navigability.

Not all who visited the river and canyon had good or exciting things to report. Lt. Ives *slightly* misjudged the future of the region. His report to army officials stated: "Ours has been the first and will doubtless be the last party of whites to visit this profitless locality. It seems intended by nature that the Colorado River, along the greater portion of its lonely and majestic way, shall be forever unvisited and undisturbed."

Ives didn't even know that white men had seen the canyon centuries earlier. He would undoubtedly blush if he knew that today the Grand Canyon attracts three million visitors a year, and is America's most popular lure.

Major John W. Powell, a geologist and authority on irrigation, made an eventful trip down the Colorado River through the canyon in 1869. Two years later he made another trip, and information gathered on these two daring experiences brought Powell fame if not fortune.

Virtually every record, every unknown, every thrill has been attempted in this spiritual place, which if uncontrolled, could become one of the greatest midways on the face of the earth. For instance, the river has been assaulted by numerous adventurers; some have floated down in life jackets or inner tubes, others powered their way down stream in home-made contraptions while others have run upstream in jet boats.

In 1937, the Museum of Natural History sponsored an investigation of Shiva Temple, a 4000 foot high "island" inside the Grand Canyon, to determine if this landmark, isolated millions of years ago by erosion, might still be occupied by primitive plant and animal life. The tour succeeded in reaching the 300 acre mesa, and found ordinary plants, ordinary animal tracks, defined bones from deer and Indian artifacts.

Oh yes, I almost forgot, they found something else—a used Kodak film carton.

In 1970, Bill Moyes, an Australian, gathered a party of witnesses, then leaped into the air from the South Rim, and eventually floated down to Phantom Ranch at the bottom—with a hang glider. He was fined $150 for "holding a special event" in a national park without a permit.

Evel Knievel proposed to "jump" a relatively narrow part of the canyon with a rocket-powered vehicle. The Park Service turned him down, so he tried to leap the Snake River in Idaho, a lesser feat, and failed.

But for every bizarre escapade or adventure in the Grand Canyon, there are tens of thousands of emotional experiences for people willing to observe park rules, whether it be to hike down and back on an approved trail, or to merely stand on a rim in awe. This is perhaps more mindful of the way Teddy Roosevelt felt about the great canyon, which he visited in 1903. "Do nothing to mar its grandeur. Keep it for your children, your children's children, and all who come after you, as the one great sight which every American should see."

Man in Arizona

The earliest evidence of man in Arizona has been found in two areas of the state. Emil Haury, an internationally known archaeologist from the University of Arizona, directed a study of Ventana Cave on the Papago Indian Reservation 100 miles west of Tucson in 1940. Haury's team found bones of large animals and killing tools suggesting that man lived in Arizona as early as 10 to 12 thousand years ago.

Approximately another 100 miles from Tucson, near the Mexican border town of Naco, another group of archaeologists uncovered the large skeleton of a mammoth and found spear points near the shoulder and head of the animal. Tests told that the animal was slain about 11 thousand years ago.

These two discoveries are the earliest records of man's appearance in Arizona. Yet, I've been around long enough to know that scientists are continually revising dates for man's existence on this planet.

With the disappearance of large animals at the close of the Ice Age several thousand years ago, civilization, which was previously on a nomadic life, had to make some profound adjustments. Early residents of Arizona, for example, were forced into becoming food gatherers—gathering and eating wild plants and cultivating or farming squash and beans.

The change from hunter to gatherer also saw a change in life-style. Instead of a roaming or nomadic existence, man began to settle into permanent living sites to tend their crops. By the time of Christ, three distinct cultures became identifiable in Arizona. Not so surprising, these three cultures relate to the land forms of Arizona: desert, highlands and plateau.

The Hohokam, a Papago Indian name meaning "gone or all used up", settled into the deserts of Arizona. They constructed pit-type homes dug partially into the soil and apparently lived in single-family units.

The Mogollon people, living in the highlands of east-central Arizona, built two types of living space: pit-type homes akin to the Hohokam, and later multi-room stone structures.

The Anasazi, a Navajo name meaning "ancients", built pueblo-type structures of mud and stone on ledges beneath overhanging cliffs. The amazing pueblo-style homes were usually built into the north wall of a cliff. The cliff gave shade in the summer (call it Arizona's first air-conditioning) and warm sunshine in the winter (Arizona's first solar heating).

Ruins from these three cultures can still be seen today. Casa Grande, a four-story adobe structure, was built by the Hohokam. Today, it is a national monument located a few miles north of Coolidge in central Arizona. The structure may have been used as a granary, observatory or temple. The Park Service has erected a large metal roof to protect the ruins from the elements. The Hohokam farmed this area, using an extensive irrigation system, parts of which still exist.

The Mogollon or mountain people left ruins on the Apache Indian Reservation. The major structure is Kinishba Ruins near the town of Whiteriver.

The Anasazi left extensive pueblo ruins at Keet Seel, Batatakin and Canyon de Chelly (de shay) in Arizona, at Mesa Verde in Colorado and at Chaco Canyon in New Mexico. Between 1300 and 1400 A.D. all three cultures seemed to disappear or perhaps disperse is more appropriate. (Direct links from this early people to today's Indian tribes are tenuous. The Hohokam culture may have been the forerunner of today's Pima Indians living south of Phoenix.)

But by 1500 these early Indians had apparently abandoned their villages or homesites, leaving behind mute testimonials to their culture. Why they moved is not certain, but tree-ring dating methods indicate it may have been a period of severe drought in Arizona.

By the time white men arrived in the mid-sixteenth century, there was only a relatively small dispersed Indian population left in the state.

Exploration of Arizona

In the early 1500s, Spain conquered Mexico and much of the Mayan treasure, including gold, was carted off for the Spanish throne. The Spanish had thoughts of more gold. Rumors persisted among the Indians of Mexico that seven cities of gold existed to the north. The result was America's first gold rush.

In 1539 the Spanish governor of Mexico, intrigued by the rumors, sent Esteban, a black slave, and Fray Marcos de Niza, a priest, to head a small group to ascertain if gold really did exist in the northern region. Esteban went ahead of Fray Marcos and eventually found his way to the Zuni villages south of Gallup, N.M. and near the Arizona-New Mexico border. Esteban made a fatal mistake. He made improper advances to the Indian women of the Zuni village and was slain. Esteban's small band then beat it back to Fray Marcos telling him that Esteban had been told of the Seven Cities of Cibola, replete with hordes of gold. The priest, shocked and frightened by the news of Esteban's death, claimed to have pursued the trail and looked upon a city larger than the city of Mexico. It is doubtful that he did anything but rush back to the gover-

nor. The Spanish leader, perhaps suspicious of the priest's integrity, sent out another small expedition to check the good father's story. They found nothing to substantiate Marcos de Niza's claim. But before they had a chance to report this news to the governor, the Spanish ruler had prepared a major expedition to be led by Don Francisco Vasquez de Coronado.

Coronado's entourage consisted of 336 soldiers, a thousand Indian allies, 1500 horses and mules and some cattle and sheep. Coronado's trail led through present-day Arizona to the Zuni villages . . . and discovered no gold whatsoever. A confrontation between Zuni villagers and Coronado's soldiers soon developed. The Zunis were overwhelmed. The battle, though a rather minor event on the expedition, did mark the first war between Indian natives and white men.

While recovering from the wounds received in the skirmish, Coronado learned from the Zunis that there were seven villages to the northwest, a region known as Tusayan. We know today that the Tusayan villages were the mesa homes of the Hopi.

Coronado sent a small detachment to investigate. The Hopis (their name means "peaceful people") temporarily forgot their manners and gave the Spanish visitors a cold welcome. A minor struggle occurred, and again there was no gold to be found.

The Hopis told of a vast river to the west, and led a small force of the Spanish to what is known now as the Grand Canyon. They were not impressed. After several unsuccessful trips to descend to the river, the expeditionary force returned to Coronado with the discouraging news. The Spanish leader, frustrated by attempts to find gold in the Arizona region, turned his attention northeastward, eventually leading his troops as far as present day Nebraska.

The Spanish search for gold ended in failure, but ironically these explorers blindly marched over rich veins of silver and copper which would only be uncovered three centuries later.

Forty years intervened before the Spanish again entered the Southwest. In 1582 a mining expedition came through the Rio Grande Valley in what is now New Mexico, then turned west into Arizona where they found ore in the Verde Valley area, between Phoenix and Flagstaff. But due to remoteness of the area, the mineral seekers ignored the ore body and returned to Mexico. Only two other brief mining expeditions came into Arizona again, one in 1598 and another in 1604.

The Spanish first came to the Southwest in search of gold, but their second entrada was for God. They found the New Mexico region easy to colonize and Christianize. By the mid-1600s several missions had been established in the lower and middle reaches of the Rio Grande region. In addition the missionaries successfully opened missions among the Hopis in northeastern Arizona, missions from San Diego to Texas, and missions in the southern part of what is now Arizona.

During this period, the pueblo natives in New Mexico grew unhappy with the successes of the white missionaries. They were obviously a threat to their religious tradition handed down from one generation to the next. Even the Hopis, though temporarily satisfied with the new religion, became restless, fearing tribal elders who recognized that the traditional "Hopi way" was endangered. So when the New Mexico pueblo people revolted, Hopis were quick to follow, and the four missionary priests in the Hopi villages were killed.

The Spanish were more successful in the southern part of Arizona in the late 1600s. Several missionaries distinguished themselves in their work with the Pima and Papago Indians. Eusebio Francisco Kino, a brilliant and energetic Jesuit missionary, spent 26 years establishing 29 missions in and around southern Arizona and northern Mexico. In 1696 he founded a mission at Tumacacori (the remains of which are a national monument today) and four years later, established a mission southeast of Tucson at a place known as Bac. Nearly a century later, a permanent church was erected at the site. Known as San Xavier del Bac, the beautiful structure is visited by thousands each year, and still serves the Papago people living in the vicinity.

Kino reasoned that the natives would be more attracted to Christianity if through it he could show them a better way of life all around. He successfully introduced farming to the Pimas and Papagos by demonstrating how to raise crops and animals. His prediction was correct: he attracted a large following to his church.

After Kino's death in 1711, relations between the Indians and the Spanish authorities deteriorated, culminating in a revolt against the Crown in 1751 in which approximately 100 settlers were slain. A year later, a *presidio* for protection was located at an area known today as Tubac, generally considered to be the first white settlement in Arizona.

With the close of this period church domination of Arizona's Indian population came to an end.

In 1767 the King of Spain expelled the Jesuit Order from Spanish lands. It was a European problem, and had nothing to do with colonization of Arizona. A year later, Franciscan missionaries arrived to take their place, the most notable was Francisco Tomás Garcés.

Garcés had real impact on the Christianization and settlement of southern Arizona. He helped explore routes to the Pacific Ocean. He also renewed contact with the Hopis. In doing so, he traveled north, saw the Grand Canyon and ended up at the Hopi village of Oraibi on July 4, 1776 (Oraibi is considered the oldest, continuously inhabited village in North America, dating back to about 1200).

The Colorado River Crossing at Yuma proved to be his undoing. It had been a growing trouble spot because of clashes between the Yuman Indians and whites over crossing the river into California. In 1781, after increasing abuse, they finally reacted by killing 55 whites, including Father Garcés.

The Yumans were not the only problems faced by white settlers. The Apaches continually raided the Santa Cruz Valley; including Tubac and the mission at Tumacacori. In the north, the Navajos also resisted the white invasion. Several decades later, in 1810, Mexico began fighting for its independence from Spain. They won 11 years later formally ending the domination of Spain and Christianity in Arizona.

The United States successfully warred with Mexico in 1848, and was ceded the northern half of the Arizona region. It would be called part of the New Mexico Territory. Six years later, the U.S. bought the southern half of Arizona as a result of the Gadsden Purchase in 1853, bringing the entire area to be called Arizona under U.S. rule.

In the 1850s, settlers asked Congress to create a separate territory for Arizona. Their requests were ignored. Then the Confederacy came into being, and many Arizona leaders wanted to join the South, where many of them had roots. A delegate was chosen to attend the Confederate Congress, and the South responded by sending troops to occupy New Mexico and Arizona areas. A small encounter between the U.S. forces and the confederates took place at Picacho Pass north of Tucson in 1862. The skirmish was called the "westernmost civil war battle". The Confederates actually won the conflict, but because their detachment was so small, the group left the territory shortly thereafter. But despite not having troops in the field, the Confederacy created the Confederate Territory of Arizona. The measure had virtually no meaning for Union troops were in charge.

The Confederate action had one significant result, however —the Congress finally created separate territorial status for Arizona and John Goodwin was named governor. Territorial headquarters were set up at Prescott in early 1864.

Arizona was still very much a frontier. Apaches were repeatedly raiding settlers in Tucson and Tubac areas, stealing food and weapons primarily, but if you got in the way you were as good as dead. In the north, the nomadic Navajos resented settlers and skirmishes were a daily occurrence, until the federal government sent in troops in 1863, headed by Kit Carson, to corral the Navajos. It was a cruel and unpleasant task. Carson was ordered to destroy their crops and livestock and force them into submission. Many hid out but eventually 8000 Indians were corraled and exiled 400 miles to Fort Sumner, southeast of Santa Fe. Most of the Navajos were forced to walk with only the sick and crippled allowed to ride in wagons. In history this event was called "The Long Walk."

For four years the Navajos were penned up at the fort, where nearly 2000 died from a smallpox epidemic. Finally, as protests to Congress mounted, they were allowed to return to their homeland in northeastern Arizona.

The proud Navajos, calling themselves *Dine*, meaning the people, struggled to regain their former life-style with some government aid to restore their sheep and goat population.

The peaceful Hopis who lived in the middle of the Navajo area, atop mesas in pueblo-like structures, were frequently raided by the Navajos. Even today conflict exists over land rights involving the Navajo and Hopi reservation.

The Apaches continued their raiding even after the Civil War. In fact, it probably increased as more settlers came into Arizona. They made hundreds of raids on small villages and ranches in the southeast section of the state led by famous warriors, two of whom were Cochise and Geronimo.

In 1861, George Bascom, a bravado Army officer, tried to capture Cochise, Chief of the Chiricahua Apaches, under a flag of truce. Cochise was wrongfully accused of kidnapping a white youth. When he denied the charge, Bascom tried to seize him. Cochise ripped open a tent and escaped. His relatives were not so lucky. Bascom held them hostage.

To retaliate, Cochise captured three employees of the Butterfield Overland Stage Company. Later, an attempt to exchange hostages failed, so Cochise swiftly killed the three. When Bascom's troops found the bodies, they promptly countered Cochise's actions by hanging the Apache hostages.

This was one of the most tragic events in U.S.-Apache dealings, it sent Cochise on a bloody rampage. Within two months after the Bascom incident, Cochise's forces had killed 150 whites. For the next ten years, the very mention of the name Cochise brought fear into the hearts of settlers.

Finally, in 1871, Thomas Jeffords, an understanding anglo who had earned Cochise's trust, led General O. O. Howard to Cochise's hiding place for a meeting. Cochise, perhaps weary from running, raiding and killing, accepted Howard's offer to move to a reservation for the Apaches. Cochise moved his followers there and died on the reservation in 1874. According to his instructions family members took his body into the Chiricahua Mountains and buried him in a secret place.

His remains have never been found.

Not one single photo exists of Cochise, but his name is recognized around the world, over a hundred years later.

Geronimo, on the other hand, was not a hereditary chief, but led a band of Chiricahua Apaches who operated mostly out of Mexico. For years his warriors raided and plundered Mexican settlements and made hit and run attacks in the Tombstone and Tucson areas.

In March of 1886, Geronimo agreed to meet with General George Crook to discuss surrender. Geronimo, upon meeting Crook, said, "Two or three words are enough. I have little to say. I surrender myself to you." Geronimo and his band were then ordered to go to the San Carlos Indian agency some 90 miles to the north. On the trip, a Tucson bootlegger sold Geronimo some whiskey. Fortified with the liquor, Geronimo and some of his warriors fled again into Mexico.

The escape cost Crook his job.

But, in September of the same year, Geronimo surrendered again to General Nelson Miles, and the Apache fear ended.

Geronimo's group, including women and children, were shipped to Florida hoping to erase their influence and snap their spirit. Later they were moved to Fort Sill, Oklahoma.

In 1903, Geronimo was converted to Christianity. He posed for pictures at expositions for small fees. Some of the images showed him attempting to look fierce, always with a weapon in hand. It was a profit-motivated stunt.

A photo taken at Theodore Roosevelt's inauguration in Washington, D.C. in 1905 by Edward Sheriff Curtis shows Geronimo a beaten, wrinkled man. His spirit was gone. Four years later he died at Fort Sill, and was buried there.

Reflecting from our historical vantage point, both sides in the Apache-settler conflict were guilty of barbaric conduct. Citizens on the Arizona frontier had adopted an attitude that "the only good Apache is a dead Apache." This led to a shameful incident in 1871, perhaps one of white man's darkest days in Arizona. No single incident prompted the event that took place that year. A citizen's group from Tucson, seeking revenge wherever and whenever they could, decided to attack a group of Apaches living near Camp Grant east of Tucson. The group hired Papagos to do the dirty work, slaying 140 Apaches, mostly women and children.

The event shocked Washington, and President Grant ordered the guilty Tucsonans brought to trial. The whites were acquitted. There was not a juror in the area who would convict a white for killing an Apache, feelings were that strong.

A solution to "The Indian Problem," was attempted as early as the 1850s when the Department of Indian Affairs (now the Bureau of Indian Affairs) was formed. Indian agents were assigned to numerous posts throughout the nation, including Arizona. The establishment of reservations followed, when the Gila River Indian Reservation was formed in 1859. Not only were the Indians losing their land, but they were being forced onto reservations and told how to live. Then came a plan to provide individual land allotments, rather than collective ownership through the tribes. The Indians did not adjust to the private ownership scheme for it simply was not "the Indian way." This system eventually failed, and many of the parcels of land were turned over to the whites.

The government next sought to aid Indians by issuing food, clothing, tools and other supplies, all of which tended to blend the Indian into our society. It created a dependency upon the government, a carry-over which is still felt today.

The Indian Reorganization Act of 1934 finally sought to involve Indians in planning and administrating federal Indian programs, something previously done solely by anglos. The program has achieved considerable success. Most tribes in Arizona now have strong tribal leadership, working in harmony with state and federal agencies.

Not everything attempted by the federal government on behalf of the American Indian has been a failure. Education and medical programs have been tremendously successful in Arizona and elsewhere. The over-riding effect, though, is to assimilate the Indian into anglo society—something not universally accepted by Indians today, particularly some of the aggressive young.

Territorial Progress

Once the fear of Indian raids were over, settlers and miners could concentrate on building, farming and mining. Even during the period of Apache raids, miners flocked to Tombstone in search of silver. The town got its name when Ed Schieffelin set out to search for silver in the area. He was admonished by friends, "All you'll find out there is your tombstone." They referred to the Apache threat. But Apaches or not, Schieffelin staked his claim and the town flourished up through the 1890s, when shafts began flooding with water.

Tombstone was tough all right, but so were Bisbee, Jerome and a host of other mining towns. But a town with a name like Tombstone has got to have some romanticism to go along with it. Yes, there really were people like Virgil, Morgan and Wyatt Earp. Their cohort, Doc Holliday, a dentist, came to the frontier and drilled more people than teeth. They fought a group of cattle rustlers in the west's most celebrated gunfight on October 26, 1881, near, *not at* the O.K. Corral in Tombstone. Things got so bad that President Chester A. Arthur deemed placing the town under martial law. But a new,

no-nonsense sheriff, John H. Slaughter, cleaned up the town.

Historians, professional and amateur, some of them among the 2000 residents of Tombstone today, still argue over the exact location of the celebrated gunfight, the duration of the skirmish, the number of shots fired and the extent of the injuries, etc. Most of the town's people good naturedly enjoy the argument, but I've often felt that the next major gunfight in Tombstone may be among the historians.

But life in Arizona in the 1880s and 1890s wasn't all movie material. People struggled with mining claims. Some made it. Others drifted to new mining camps, hoping to strike it rich. A typical work week in an underground mine involved a 10-hour day, six days a week. And there were other non-romantics, like housewives, barbers, businessmen . . . none of whom carried weapons.

Gold and silver weren't the only mining lures in Arizona. By 1880 a sizable copper mining industry developed and today, Arizona leads the nation in copper output.

Ranching was also a large-scale business in Arizona by 1880. The grasslands of southeastern Arizona, above the Mogollon Rim and the Colorado plateau were areas where major ranches developed. Many of them exist today. The arrival of the railroads in this period greatly aided the ranching industry which could then ship beef east to the major population centers at relatively cheap rates.

Cowboys developed out of the ranching industry and enjoyed their share of romanticism, movies have made sure of that. One of the most amusing definitions of a cowboy and an anonymous one at that, it retold by Arizona historian Marshall Trimble:

"You ask me what cowboys is? I'll tell you what cowboys is. Cowboys is noisey fellers with bow legs and brass stomachs that works from the hurricane deck of a Texas broomtail and hates any kind of work that can't be done atop one. They lives in and loves the outdoors, hates fences and respects rivers. They can spit ten feet into a stiff wind, cuss like muleskinners, ride like Comanches and rope like Mexicans—and independent, why you throw one of um into a raging river and he'll just naturally float upstream."

Despite the rip-roaring Saturday nights in Bisbee or Tombstone, there were serious politicians in Tucson, Phoenix and Prescott mounting a strong movement for statehood. Congress was stubborn, but in 1905 and 1906 it considered bills which provided for one large state from the territories of Arizona and New Mexico. The proposed name for the combined state was "Arizona the Great!" But Arizonans obviously wanted their own state, for voters turned down both proposals. Then President Theodore Roosevelt backed the joint state idea with the capital earmarked for Santa Fe. Phoenix residents became indignant and promptly changed Roosevelt Street to Cleveland Street (They recanted years later; today there is a Roosevelt Street). In 1910, Congress allowed Arizonans to draft a constitution and apply for statehood. But President William H. Taft vetoed the bill because of a clause allowing for recall of judges by a vote. The clause was stricken from the constitution and the way was paved for statehood.

On January 6, 1912, President Taft signed a bill admitting New Mexico as the 47th state. Eight days later, on Valentine's Day, Taft signed the documents making Arizona the 48th.

The changes in Arizona since statehood have been dramatic. If we consider only the period from the end of World War II to the end of the 1970s, the growth has been explosive.

Population of Arizona at the time of statehood was right at 210,000. By 1960 it was 1.3 million then rose to 1.7 million in 1970 and at the turn of this decade, Arizona's population is 2.5 million. It has been one of the three fastest growing states in population since the 1960s.

What accounts for Arizona's tremendous growth? Climate has been a major attraction. When air-conditioning became widespread in the 1950s, the desert population centers of Phoenix and Tucson, always pleasant places to be in the winter, becoming downright tolerable during the summer.

During the war, Arizona's skies were filled with aircraft from numerous bases providing pilot training for the Army Air Corps. Many of the GIs liked what they saw in Arizona during the war and returned to live there.

Tourism has been a major industry and continues to grow at an accelerating pace. With tourism, a certain growth factor results, for those who choose Arizona as a vacation spot are also apt to want to live there permanently. Also, the lure of retirement living in Arizona has rendered its share of growth.

The state has attracted many new industries, too. Manufacturing has now replaced agriculture and mining as the state's chief source of income.

Arizona, however, faces one major problem as far as continued growth is concerned—water supply. The problem has been with this land as long as it was a desert. Tucson is the largest American city relying solely on underground water supplies. The water table there is dropping at an alarming rate. Yet, the city has grown to 400,000 and continues to soak up water. It can't continue this trend forever.

The Phoenix metropolitan area, with a population approaching 1.5 million, obtains its water from wells and the Salt River Project, the massive reclamation program that brings water from the mountains into the city and outlying agricultural areas by means of an irrigation canal system. Long range needs for this thirsty metropolis may be satisfied by the $1.5 billion Central Arizona Project, which will bring water to the valley from the Colorado River in the northwest corner of the state through an aqueduct. As a consequence of the growing water needs, dropping water tables and land subsidence, there are those who predict doom for Arizona's population centers. They warn philosophically that the desert was meant to be a desert, and attempts to turn it into a green carpet for homes, golf courses, agriculture and other water using amenities have to end somewhere.

There is reason for alarm. But doom? I don't know. But I do know that effective leadership at the state and city level must come to grips with the matter.

Or else.

A Treasure Chest

Arizona's history is rich. So is its bounty of natural wonders. So much, that has made Arizona a fascinating state, is preserved by the National Park Service. The two national parks in Arizona are the Grand Canyon and the Petrified Forest-Painted Desert, discussed earlier. But there are also 14 national monuments in Arizona, not equalled by any other state.

A trip here is a lesson in Arizona's past and present.

Indian ruins make up eight of the 14 monuments. In the northern part of the state is Navajo National Monument containing remote pueblo dwellings known as Keet Seel and Betatakin. On the eastern border is Canyon de Chelly, an awesome canyon dotted with majestic ruins left by the Anasazi.

In the north-central region around Flagstaff are Wupatki and Walnut Canyon ruins. A few miles northeast of Flagstaff is Sunset Crater, a major volcanic cone which exploded a thousand years ago. The area around the crater is still strewn with volcanic debris.

Between Flagstaff and Phoenix are two more ruins; Montezuma Castle and Tuzigoot. East of Phoenix is Tonto National Monument, a major ruin above Roosevelt Lake.

The Casa Grande National Monument is a four-story adobe building abandoned by the Hohokam several centuries ago. Tumacacori Mission is located just north of Nogales and is a reminder of those days when Christianity first came into the state. West of Nogales, 100 miles along the Mexican border, is Organ Pipe Cactus National Monument, a preserve where one may drive through stands of the unusual cactus. On the east and west sides of Tucson are the two sections of Saguaro National Monument. It is unique that Arizona should have two monuments for cactus.

In the southeast portion of the state is the Chiricahua National Monument, an array of rocks, and former home for the warriors following Cochise and Geronimo in the 1800s.

And finally, on the Utah-Arizona border is Pipe Spring National Monument, a tribute to pioneering days in the state.

Arizona is Indian Country! There are 21 reservations in Arizona accounting for 26.6 percent of the land area, or more than 20 million acres. If that seems like a large amount of Indian land, remember that prior to the arrival of anglos, the Indians owned it all.

Arizona also has the highest Indian population of any state. There are 14 different tribes, accounting for 140,000 people living on reservations. There are also an unknown number, probably less than 10,000 living off the reservation land, mostly in Arizona's towns or cities.

The Navajo Reservation, most of which is in Arizona, is the largest tribal unit in the country. It covers 15 million acres or about 25,000 square miles, equating size of West Virginia.

The Papago Reservaton in southern Arizona is the second largest in the state and the country, with 2.7 million acres.

Arizona Navajos are something special. Their land is fascinating. Indian ruins, trading posts, canyons, mountains, forests, lakes, desert with sand dunes and sandstone monuments, and thousands of hogans (the traditional Navajo home made of wood, brush and mud) dot the sprawling region.

The Navajo are known the world over for their fine silver, gold, and turquoise jewelry and colorful and unique rugs. The tribe proudly calls its people and land "The Navajo Nation."

Right in the middle of the Navajo land is the Hopi Reservation composed of about 7000 tribal members. A "traditional" Hopi, is one who lives by the "Hopi way"—a strict, complicated and admirable religious life-style. The Hopi crafts of silversmithing, basketry and pottery are well known for their beauty and symbolism.

A buffer zone separates the Hopi and Navajo reservations. It was established in the 1930s to allow Hopis and Navajos to share a Joint-Use Area. The old Navajo-Hopi conflict, dating back two or three centuries, is still alive. Court battle after court battle have been waged . . . tempers have flared . . . cattle have been shot. The conflict is not merely over land use, but life itself. Some of the tribal members are to be relocated in accordance with a settlement arranged by the Bureau of Indian Affairs. But these people do not want to be moved. Their land is a very important part of their life.

It is a most unfortunate struggle for the Navajo and Hopi, for they are a truly beautiful people!

The most remote and unusual reservation is that of the Havasupai Indians, consisting of 325 members living deep in a canyon west of the Grand Canyon Village. The tribe owns 188,000 acres, accessible to the outside world only by foot, horse, or helicopter.

Each tribe in Arizona has their own unique features, but the lands of the Navajo, Hopi and Havasupai are especially scenic which attract throngs of visitors. The Hopi and Navajo reservations have motels, restaurants, and service stations. Because this region is deceivingly large, motel reservations and advance planning are necessary before entering.

It is also imperative that visitors realize they are guests and should conduct themselves accordingly. Most tribes have regulations regarding visitors which have come about because of abused privileges. One example is photography within the Hopi villages. It is absolutely forbidden. When in doubt, ask about tribal policies.

Indians add a special dimension to Arizona. They are fascinating and interesting . . . just like the land they live on. The bond between these people and the beautiful Arizona land is poetically expressed in this old Navajo chant.

"Beauty before me,
beauty behind me,
beauty below me,
beauty above me,
beauty all around me."

View from Yaki Point on the South Rim of Grand Canyon
National Park. That magic moment as the sun slowly departs
leaving this indelible memory in its wake.

Above: Forces of nature define the giants of the desert in their
protected area, Saguaro National Monument. In background,
the Santa Catalina Mountains. Right: Tucked between walls
of Palm Canyon in the Kofa Mountains grow
the state's only native palms.

Above: Evening primrose and sand verbena burst forth
following a gentle rain, near Bullhead City along
the Colorado River. Left: Erosion creates unique patterns
on the sandstone walls of upper Antelope Canyon near Page.

Buds erupt from tip of arm on giant Saguaro. This creamy white
flower opens after sundown in late May or June and then
closes forever in a day or so.

Goldpoppies and phacelia temper the severity of volcanic
boulders on a desert slope near Wikieup. Pages 24 and 25
following: Yebechai rocks form dramatic background
as a family of Navajos take their flock of sheep and goats
to nearby spring.

Polychrome bowl made by prehistoric people who lived
in what is now called the ruins of Kinishba,
on Fort Apache Indian Reservation.

Above: An aura of mystery hovers over sandstone buttes
as approaching storm and evening shadows unite
in Monument Valley. Pages 28 and 29 following:
The setting sun brightens the surface of Lake Havasu.

Above: Conifers contrast with carpet of fall foliage and white
aspen trees, near east rim of Grand Canyon.
Right: Golden tones of autumn reign supreme
in aspen grove of Kaibab National Forest.

Above: Evening primrose adds a special feeling to soil patterns
in the desert following a heavy rain. Left: Ancient land forms
beneath an overlay of volcanic activity rising from
Kingman Wash, near Hoover Dam.

Rocky Mountain maple foliage carpets the forest floor
in northern area of state.

Deer Creek cut this spectacular gorge through red sandstone,
prior to making a 200 foot drop to join the Colorado River.

Aerial view of southwest desert area reveals result of rare
torrential rains, causing erosion of the softer soil.

Lower Granite Gorge of the Colorado River viewed from point
in Hualapai Indian Reservation. The river forms the boundary
between Indian lands and Grand Canyon National Park.

View in Coal Canyon reveals break-off from Moenkopi Mesa
on Colorado Plateau in Navajo Indian Reservation.

Above: Spider Rock soars 800 feet from the floor of
Canyon de Chelly National Monument creating an awesome
formation. Pages 40 and 41 following: Weather-worn juniper
frames a broad view of erosion scarred Monument Valley.

Cereus blossoms reflect the adaptability of this cactus plant
to the southwest, following its importation from South America.

Above: Another aspect of the rare beauty of the Joshua tree
is delineated as the sun rises along eastern edge
of Mojave desert. Pages 44 and 45 following: Stormy sky
casts an ominous glow over striated columns on the Colorado
Plateau, in Navajo Indian land.

Snow covered pinyon tree at Mojave Point on the South Rim
appears to be in complete harmony with low clouds
covering the distant North Rim.

Early autumn snow on 12,670 foot San Francisco Peaks,
highest point in the state.

Above: Lone cottonwood tree looms tall as the sun disappears
at Quitobaquito Oasis, in Organ Pipe Cactus National
Monument. Right: Carpet of gold poppies and blue lupine
signal the arrival of spring in valley of the Black Mountains.

Above: Chain-fruit cholla frames the rugged Ajo Mountains, in Organ Pipe Cactus National Monument. Left: Prickly poppies soften the towering red Vermillion Cliffs standing just north of the Marble Gorge of the Colorado River.

Above: Lichen, covering volcanic rocks and prickly pear cactus,
appear equally hardy in the sun drenched region
of the lower Verde Valley. Right: Sea of red sand is perfect
setting for the delicate spring flowers of the pentstemon,
at base of Echo Cliffs, on the Colorado Plateau.

Above: Cottonwood trees achieve their maximum beauty during
autumn in the semi arid lands of the southwest. Left: Dramatic
view at junction of Canyon de Chelly and Canyon del Muerto,
bares water cut gorges famed for scenic, prehistoric ruins
and summer home for Navajo Indians. Pages 56 and 57
following: Sandstone cliffs and rising summer thunderhead
blend to create a special view across Wahweap Bay,
on Lake Powell, in Glen Canyon National Recreation Area.

Above: Piercing rays of the morning sun delivers an awesome
outline of Wotan's Throne and Vishnic Temple, in Grand Canyon
National Park. Right: Wintry sky is the perfect background
for tall grass as it resists the force of a gentle breeze.

Above: Section of petrified tree balances on slowly eroding
bentonitic clay pedestal, in Petrified Forest National Park.
Left: Slabs of petrified wood now fully exposed after shedding
their coat of clay, in Petrified Forest National Park.

Above: Petroglyphs etched in these basalt boulders prompted
the state to establish Painted Rocks Historic Park, near Gila Bend.
Right: Interior of Poncho House ruins cleverly stabilized
on sloping rock near east rim of Monument Valley.

Above: Remnants of pueblo village on limestone ridge
overlooking fertile Verde River Valley, in Tuzigoot National
Monument. Left: Elderly cottonwood tree acquires
an unusual autumn hue during a sun-filled moment
against a brilliant blue sky.

Giant saguaros and prickly pear cactus dominate mouth
of Aravaipa Canyon in Galiuro Mountains.

Muted winter sunset makes a dramatic entry in late afternoon
to highlight bare trees and snow on Bill Williams Mountain.

Clump of beavertail cactus and joshua trees create a perfect
arrangement, along Pierce Ferry Road, in Mojave County.

Red orb of the setting sun heralds end of the day as a cloudburst
descends upon the desert near Tucson.

Young patient sits beside the ornate design used as an altar,
in a healing ritual. The medicine man at the left chants as
his helper uses a rattle in an ancient Navajo ceremony,
still performed by the tribe on their reservation.

Above: Colorfully wrapped dead birds are utensils still used
by the Navajo Indian medicine man, to work supernatural
powers, to purify the patient. Pages 72 and 73 following:
Antelope pictographs, etched in red sandstone walls
by prehistoric dwellers, on the Navajo Indian Reservation.

Above: Solid carpet of poppies and stately saguaro create
a vivid spring arrangement along the Apache Trail,
in Tonto National Monument. Right: Famous saguaros
loom tall at base of Superstition Mountain, site of the
Lost Dutchman's Mine and disappearing prospectors.

Above: Perhaps nature's most brilliant spring awakening
is the Mariposa lily, eyed in Dripping Springs Mountains.
Left: Shrine of Santa Rita appears well guarded by two
aged saguaros on the desert east of Tucson.
Holes are the handiwork of Gila woodpeckers.

Above: Yucca plants unveil their flowering cycle during
the month of June. In background stand the rugged
Santa Catalina Mountains. Right: Colorful baskets reveal
the tasteful talents of the Hopi Indians.

Above: Sunlight enhances the rare beauty of this cactus bloom
at the peak of maximum development. Left: The artistry
and skill of a Navajo Indian is unfolding as one more rug
nears completion via her hand-made loom.

Above: Verdant saguaro and prickly pear cacti frame
the brilliant white St. Augustine Cathedral, erected in 1897.
It is the heart of the "Old Pueblo" as Tucson is affectionately
called. Right: Butterfly at ease on tip of blooming Agave
cactus, standing tall in green forest of the Pinaleno Mountains.

Above: Seemingly endless bands of color occupy the eye
on Blue Mesa, in Petrified Forest National Park.
Left: Sand dunes assume intriguing shapes from the billowing
wind as it moves with limited interference across
Monument Valley.

Cliffrose tends to ease the stark appearance of Full Moon Arch
formed on face of sandstone cliff, in Monument Valley.

Above: The Salt River flows placidly along base of colored
ledges formed by mineral bearing springs, in Fort Apache
Indian Reservation. Pages 88 and 89 following: Late afternoon
sunlight seemingly warms the carpet of snow at base
of Sentinel Mesa, in Monument Valley.

Above: Winter rains transform desert into a carpet of
wildflowers, such as owlclover, lupine and golden poppy.
The rugged Ajo Mountains anchor the background. Right: May
and June herald the arrival of Organ Pipe cactus blossoms in
Organ Pipe Cactus National Monument. A species limited to
this area, forms a fruit savored by both Indians and birds.

Above: The Civic Plaza in downtown Phoenix, is indicative
of the tasteful development shaping this growing metropolis.
Left: One of the first flowers of spring seen in the desert
is the colorful beavertail cactus.

Cascading water of Salt River destined to fulfill the needs
of Phoenix, and the fertile Valley of the Sun.

Giant meteorite left this indelible mark on the desert area
of northern Arizona. Crater measures 570 feet deep
and approximately three miles around.

Autumn-flowering rabbitbrush dots the surface of a dry wash
on the Colorado Plateau, near Fredonia.

Cholla cactus offers a change of pace on the Sonoran Desert,
dominated by serrated Kofa Mountains in background.

Above: Spring run-off in Sycamore Creek from the Mazatzal
Mountains northeast of Phoenix. Wild blooming rhubarb
adds to the season's excitement. Right: Autumn tinged leaves
in foreground tend to soften the dramatic shape
of Cathedral Rocks, in Oak Creek Canyon.

Above: Grand Falls of the Little Colorado River, reflecting
the effect of heavy rains in the upper basin. This usually dry
river bed fills to capacity following a storm, creating
a chocolate colored Niagara in the desert.
Left: The first signs of winter create a spectacular contrast
with evergreens and aspen in Kaibab National Forest.

Lacy autumn foliage of saltcedar renders unique variation with
the smooth bentonitic clay hills in a dry wash, near Cameron.

Above: Peak of the blooming season is at hand in cactus garden
of Southwestern Arboretum, near Superior. Pages 104 and 105
following: At days end the sun illuminates a band of clouds
casting a faint reflection on grove of cacti, west of Tucson.

Row of autumn draped poplars stand as silent monarchs
deep in the heart of Oak Creek Canyon.

Above: Sunlight and green foliage adds serenity to this hidden
retreat, in Granite Dells. Pages 108 and 109 following:
Silhouette of whip-like ocotillos and distant crags, mark floor
of Sonoran Desert, as the sun and thunderhead cloud perform.

Reasonably modern Hopi pueblo house near Oraibi. The Hopis
are the only Pueblo Indians in the state, still clinging
to their ancient customs.

Fall foliage of aspen trees and rustic fence reflected
on mirror-like surface of small pond in Kaibab National Forest.

Above: Lava rocks and water eroded formations called
"Indian Teepees" vary the surface of lower Verde Valley.
Right: A vertical limestone cliff shelters this prehistoric
dwelling along Beaver Creek. Now designated as Montezuma's
Castle National Monument, it is ninety percent intact
containing 20 rooms. It was occupied by an agrarian
people until close to 1400 A.D.

Above: Aerial view of Havasu Canyon, a sidethrust to Grand
Canyon of the Colorado River. This region is home
of the Havasupai Indians, people of the blue-green water.
Left: Navajo Falls in Havasu Canyon at western edge of Grand
Canyon National Park. One mile upstream from these beautiful
falls is the isolated Indian village of the Havasupais.

Above: Winter's generous mantle beautifies the summit
of Schnebly Hill, near Sedona. Right: Golden glow
of the setting sun accents cluster of conifers growing
on wind swept slope of the San Francisco Peaks.

Above: Ample snowfall clearly defines the path of this little
stream as it leaves its birthplace, in the White Mountains.
Left: Hoarfrost and fog create a breathless hushed feeling
on mid-winter day in Kaibab National Forest.
Pages 120 and 121 following: The Mittens, famous buttes
that straddle the Arizona-Utah border. They stand some
three miles apart and rise about 1,000 feet
from the floor of Monument Valley.

Rich desert color is fully expressed in blossoms of prickly pear
cactus as they unfold throughout the Sonoran Desert.

Above: Joshua tree announces the arrival of spring as it bursts
into bloom on the Mojave Desert. Pages 124 and 125 following:
Giant fingers of rock acquire an eerie feeling as the light
of day fades away under a full moon over Monument Valley.

Above: Eroded by forces of nature this 75 foot high sandstone
pillar stands at edge of White Mesa, overlooking Klethla Valley,
on Navajo Indian Reservation. Right: Betatakin, one of three
major prehistoric ruins, nestled against wall of red sandstone
in Navajo National Monument.

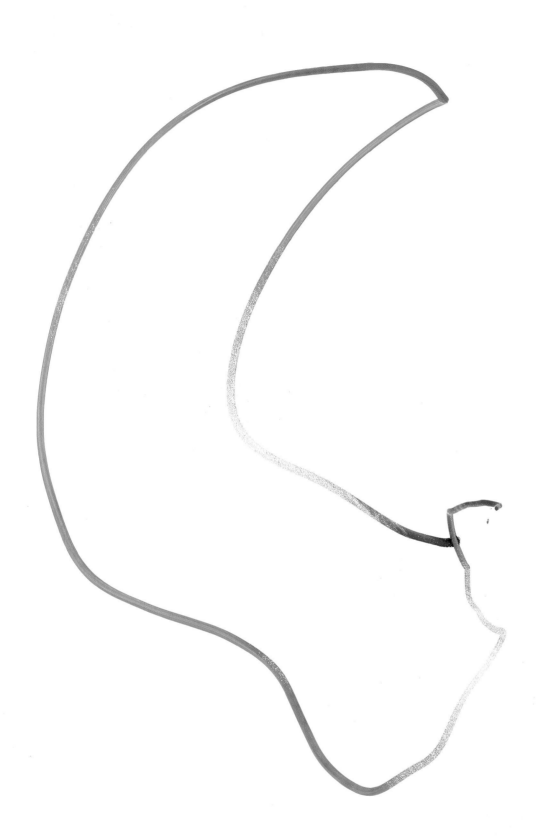